I'm Still Here by Stephanie Michels

Published by Lightning Tower Press, LLC
P.O. Box 381
Shoreham, NY 11786

Copyright © 2024 by Stephanie Michels

All rights reserved. No portion of this book may be reproduced in any form without written permission from the publisher, except as permitted by U.S. copyright law. For permissions, address Lightning Tower Press, LLC., P.O. Box 381, Shoreham, NY 11786
lightningtowerpress@gmail.com

Characters and places in this book are either a product of the author's imagination or used with the individual's permission. Photos are printed with permission from subjects.

Library of Congress Control Number:
2024946958

ISBN 979-8-9865558-2-9

Printed in the United States of America.

First Edition: 2025

5 4 3 2

I'M STILL HERE

To my sister, Katie,
who continues to be my rock.

I'M STILL HERE

Written and Illustrated by
Stephanie Michels

Where do you go when you are no more? Do you go back to Earth as something new, like a butterfly or a tree? Or do you go to Heaven to be with your family?

Daisy began to stir. She felt woozy, almost as if she chased a string in a circle too many times. She felt soft grass under her back and the sun warming her belly like one of her human's warm hugs. Little bugs flew around her. Their wings made a whirring noise that sounded like music.

"Daisy," a cold nose was poking her, "wake up. It's time to go."

"Shadow? Is that you?" Daisy was awake now. Her sister's voice hadn't changed since she saw her last. "It's been years. Where have you been?"

Daisy remembered the last time she saw Shadow with their family. Their dad was gently putting her into the back of his red truck. Daisy hid under the strong smell of the lavender bushes and watched the truck pull away. Her sister didn't come back home.

Shadow was panting from the summer heat. "My soul has been resting after many years of playing. It's time for you to rest now too."

"Wait, what do you mean? I'm not ready to rest. Katie just came home." Little pricks of panic spread across Daisy's body.

The little whirring wings that once sounded so beautiful had quickly become an earache. Why did she have to leave? Katie, her human, finally came home to her. Daisy didn't understand why she wasn't with Katie.

Daisy sat down to process what Shadow told her. She looked out among the dense forest that surrounded her, and suddenly felt so small. She wished she was with her person.

"I'm not leaving. I will wait here forever for Katie to come back to me."

The smell of smoke filled the air and crickets chirped with the crackling campfire. The sun had set and the stars lit up the sky. They were at their family's camp, where they spent many days playing with their humans.

Three small children surrounded their mother as their father looked on. Shadow was lying at their father's feet. Her fur wasn't coated in old white hair. In the hands of the mother rested a small kitten. Daisy knew where they were.

"This is the day we found you in the woodpile." Shadow stared at the children. "Katie just started kindergarten then. We all knew you were coming home with us."

"Come on," Shadow said. "We have more memories to explore."

The smokey air lifted and the crickets became a whisper in the distance. Loud, shrieking laughter called the two forward. Crinkling paper, talking toys, and the slap of small feet against the floor was all Daisy could hear as they entered their family's home.

In the corner of the living room was a Christmas tree with low hanging ornaments. Daisy loved to play with them, much to their mother's dismay. The kids had grown a little more since the last memory. In the center of the excitement, sat Daisy and Katie. They were enchanted by the shoelace between them. Each time Daisy lept up, Katie would errupt in giggles. It was Daisy's favorite sound.

"I don't understand. If I'm not gone, then why am I not with her right now?" Daisy turned her attention away from her human and looked at Shadow.

"I struggled to understand that too when I left." Shadow said. "You live in her memories. Everytime she thinks of you, you're right there next to her. She can't see you, but she can feel your love deep inside her heart."

"What if she forgets me?" Daisy felt sad as she watched Katie snuggle with her past self. She wished to give Katie sandpaper kisses.

"Katie will never forget you. You two were inseparable. She loves you more than anything on Earth."

"If Katie loved me, then why did she leave?" Daisy walked by her former self sleeping peacefully on Katie's big bed.

"She didn't want to leave you. She joined the military, remember?" Shadow led the way through the memory. "No one wanted her to go, but they were all so proud of her for doing great things."

Daisy and Shadow walked along the path of memories, before appearing outside of their family's home. Snow fell around them, and they could see their breath rise above them. A chill ran down Daisy's spine.

"Look here," said Shadow as she stood against the side of the house, with two paws firmly placed against the beige panels. "She did come back to you."

Daisy eagerly peeked into the window, and saw their family laughing and hugging Katie. Tightly wrapped in her arms, resting against the camouflage sleeves, was Daisy's other self. She heard everyone telling Katie how proud they were of her.

As she stared on, Daisy felt proud of her too.

After a while they continued to walk on. The snow evaporated into puddles as they came back into the dense, warm forest. The whirring of wings began to play in Daisy's ears again.

Daisy sat at the edge of the forest for a while. The heat settled into her bones and she stared back down the path they came from. The sun was beginning to make her feel tired. However, she wasn't sure if she was ready to leave.

"Shadow," Daisy whispered, "will Katie be okay?"

Shadow perked her head up from laying on the ground and looked at Daisy. "I promise she will be fine. You're in her heart forever and always."

Daisy turned and looked at Shadow. She paused, thinking for a minute as she looked back at the memories one more time.

"I think I'm ready to rest."

Deep in her heart, she felt warm and loved. Almost as if soft whiskers brushed against her to say, "I love you forever and always."

After 15 years, on November 28th, 2022 Daisy crossed the rainbow bridge in Katie's arms. The vet said that her kidney disease wasn't going to get better. We didn't want her to be in pain.

~~Daisy didn't want Katie to let go of her. She relaxed as Katie and Dad~~ talked with her and pet her fur. They told her how much we all loved her. Katie kissed Daisy one last time.

The sun doesn't shine the same on the couch where you slept. Your fur clings to my clothes as if you were still here. I have to remind myself that you're in a better place, even if it isn't with me.

You were more than a pet to me. You were my best friend, my sister. We grew up together.

One day I'll come home to you. We'll meet at the pearly gates, just as if it was our first time meeting at the woodpile. Please wait for me.

I love you forever and always.
-Katie

www.ingramcontent.com/pod-product-compliance
Lightning Source LLC
Chambersburg PA
CBHW051326110526
44582CB00003B/67